CHURCH
HURTS
and the
HEALING
PROCESS

DOT KELLEY

WESTBOW
PRESS®
A DIVISION OF THOMAS NELSON
& ZONDERVAN

WestBow Press books may be ordered through booksellers or by contacting:

WestBow Press
A Division of Thomas Nelson & Zondervan
1663 Liberty Drive
Bloomington, IN 47403
www.westbowpress.com
1 (866) 928-1240

ISBN: 978-1-9736-4143-8 (sc)
ISBN: 978-1-9736-4142-1 (hc)
ISBN: 978-1-9736-4144-5 (e)

Library of Congress Control Number: 2018911733

Print information available on the last page.

WestBow Press rev. date: 11/13/2018

Contents

Preface...i

Chapter 1 Love Never Fails 1

Chapter 2 Don't Put Your Confidence in Man ... 17

Chapter 3 Forgive and Fulfill Your Destiny 25

Chapter 4 Wisdom—the Principle Thing..........45

Chapter 5 Obedience Is Better Than Sacrifice ... 55

Chapter 6 Spiritual Growth and Stability..........67

Chapter 7 God Is Our One and Only Source....77

Chapter 8 There Is Nothing That You
           Cannot Overcome 87

Preface

Church Hurts and the Healing Process was written to bring awareness to unchristian-like behaviors that exist in our Christian environments. I was inspired to write this book by listening to hurts of people from various churches in my work with the Follow-up Care Ministry.

This book is a heartfelt and encouraging guide that addresses conflicts in our Christian relationships. It encourages Christian believers to acquire a spirit of forgiveness and love for one another.

Thanks to Minister Larry Hall who was always there in my seasons of writing with prayer, encouragement, and giving me that extra push to finish the book. A very special thanks to Dr. Dennis Anderson who has mentored and guided me through some difficult times during my years of writing as I made efforts to follow God's chosen path for my life.

Chapter 1

LOVE NEVER FAILS

We are in a continual battle with the spiritual forces of evil and darkness, but we will triumph when we yield to walking in love. Love is the most powerful spiritual force in the universe. We were created to have a loving nature—in the image of God. Love has the power to overcome any adverse circumstances. Love never fails. "This is my commandment, that you love one another as I have loved you" (John 15:12).

When Christian believers fail to walk in love, we become victims of church hurts in our Christian environments. Love hurts, and love heals. If we love, we will be hurt. But if we hurt, we have to love all the more. We must make a choice to love beyond our pain, or we will never be restored or have lasting relationships.

Although we were created in the image of Christ, we still deal with our natural tendencies to sin that causes us to lack progress in the area of love. We allow our flesh to be reactive and we get irritated and speak unkindly when someone has insulted us or spoken negatively. We must communicate with compassion in our hearts for one another.

The more love we have in our hearts, and the more we realize we were born to love, the more fully God will be revealed in our love walk.

The ability to love is one of our greatest gifts. According to 1 Corinthians 13, Love is patient and kind, it does not envy, it does not boast, it is not easily angered, it is not proud or rude, it is not self-seeking, it does not indulge in evil. Love never fails.

If you are a victim of words spoken in a hurtful manner in a Christian relationship, it is important to quickly share your feelings with that person in order for him or her to either have the chance to apologize or to explain how you may have misunderstood his or her words or intentions. Be quick to show love and make amends with your offender. The more quickly we acknowledge our mistakes and the impact they have had on victims, the less likely they are to turn into anger and bitterness. If you do not resolve your misunderstandings, the hurtful feelings can quickly cause offense.

Love in the midst of hurt will cause you to be open-minded with the person who caused the offense. If your gesture of love is rejected, know that God will be there with His unconditional love to restore you to a peace of mind.

Church hurts are created sometimes by judging others, and judging others is commonplace in our relationships in Christian environments. Judgmental spirits will keep us in unrighteousness, causing division and separating us from God. God's Word says you will stand in judgment of every word that proceeds out of your mouth, whether good or bad (2 Corinthians 5:10).

Whether you have been wounded or rejected by Christianity, or you have unintentionally hurt people through judgments, make amends and turn the situation into a relationship that can be resolved. "Therefore, let us not judge one another anymore, but rather resolve this, not to put a stumbling block or a cause to fall in our brother's way" (Romans 14:13).

Church hurts are also created sometimes when Christian believers are unaware of how people respond to careless insults or comments. And being unaware of people's emotional states of mind when our comments are not in line with God's Word can cause resentment; consequently, we allow the resentment to linger, or the hurt caused by the actions may live on for years. This often causes the victim to acquire negative hidden emotions that sometimes can destroy or hinder your spiritual relationships.

You don't expect Christian believers to mistreat you; you expect this only from the people of the secular world. And because these Christian believers have knowledge of the word of God, their spoken words can be especially hurtful. How can we say we love God and hate our Christian brothers and sisters? "If someone says, 'I love God' and hates his brother, he is a liar; for he who does not love his brother whom he has seen, 'how can he love God who he has not seen? And this commandment we have from Him that he who loves God must love his brother also" (1 John 4:20–21).

In the midst of hurtful remarks, you must make a decision to yield to the Spirit and respond positively. Our words can wound so deeply, and our tempers can hurt those we love the most. We can't change spoken words; we only learn from them. Let your words and your actions strengthen your Christian relationships.

Your life is a reflection of the words you speak. Words are creative forces, and words have power. Our words have the power to tear down and the power to build up. The words we speak are actually what's in the heart. For those Christians whose hearts have been changed by the power of God, there should be a change reflected in their words. So, if we fill our hearts with the love of Christ, only words that enlighten or inspire will come out of our mouths.

We could prevent a lot of hurtful feelings if we would just arrange our words to convey a spirit that is sensitive to the feelings of others. By giving careful attention to how we speak beforehand, we can change our circumstances for the better. Contemplating our thoughts and words before we speak will keep us conscientious in our Christian relationships.

Choose to speak life-giving words that encourage rather than negative words that discourage. Words have the ability to help and to heal when spoken in the right context. It is how we use our words that creates the end result. It is not what we say; it is how we say it.

You often will find yourself in so many situations in life that will test your walk with God, to see what level of spiritual maturity you possess. You may experience an ungodly, challenging situation to test your faith in His Word and to see where you are in adhering to the commandments of love.

We will never understand God's plans for our lives or the paths He will lead us through to get certain character flaws corrected. God always has a plan to test our faith.

Faith connects us to the promises of God, and all of God's promises are rightfully ours when faith is activated. If there is no love for others, our prayers of faith will not work. Love makes faith work. Showing faith and love will produce a supernatural response that moves the hand of God in your circumstances.

We all go through difficult times in our relationships, but God will work things out when we make the appropriate changes in our lives and yield to love.

The benefits of walking in love are rewarding. Love keeps no record of wrongs.

In our Christian environments, our behavior should be examples for others; we should be positive role models, consistent in our spiritual walk with God. We should always take the peaceful way out. God's Word tells us what our attitudes should be toward Him and toward others. "When a man's ways please the Lord, he makes even his enemies to be at peace with him" (Proverbs 16:7).

When your new converts see the love of God in you, they will want to know what driving force is behind your attitude of love and peace. We must love others as we love ourselves; how we desire to be loved is how we should love others.

If we live our lives according to the commandment of love, no one can steal our joy. Without love, there is not any joy, and the joy of the Lord is our strength. Joy keeps you strong in the midst of your hardships. Your joy should continue to exist in unpleasant circumstances. An attitude of joy indicates faith and trust in God that He will sustain you through your difficult times.

When we stand strong on God's commandments and promises, He will always show Himself faithful. And you can rest assured that whatever God has promised, He will fulfill.

Love for Christian believers is the inseparable product of love for God. Love as Christ loved. We must seek to live each day with the love of God shed aboard in our hearts and we must be fully acquainted with the fruit of the spirit which is love, joy, peace, patience, kindness, goodness, faithfulness, gentleness and self-control. Without love in our hearts, nothing else matters. "Beloved, let us love one another, for love is of God, and everyone who loves is born of God and knows God. He who does not love does not know God, for God is love" (1 John 4:7–8).

It is easy to love and be kind to people who are loving and kind to you. The challenge comes when you know you should react in love but you have a desire to mistreat someone who has hurt you. You should pray for and bless the one who has hurt you. In doing so you will experience comfort and peace of mind. Pray for the release of the bitterness and anger you feel toward your brother or sister. Release the one who did you wrong by forgiving the person. Restore the relationship to one that demonstrates meekness and kindness. You have God's nature inside of you, and it is His nature to love and forgive.

Love is a predominant force that will aid in the healing process, and it is very effective in transformation. Through love we can heal and become whole again, and with loving actions we can experience a oneness with others. Humility is an act of love that should be displayed in our relationships. Humility means to look at your feelings as less important than the feelings of others. Humility puts the need of others before your own. If people can see how much you really care about their well-being, they will be influenced by this more than anything else to understand that your intentions are to help and not to hurt.

In many circumstances in life, we are challenged to love those who are displeasing or people who are difficult to love—the disagreeable. There are people who have experienced situations in which they felt unwanted, unloved or rejected by Christianity. They need to feel loved no matter what circumstances exist in their lives, it does not matter what they believe, it does no matter if their moral values are contrary to God's Word. Love and acceptance of others regardless of where they are in life is essential to influencing them toward faith in God. When you earn people's trust, you can help meet their needs. God loves us all the same, He shows no partiality, He loves the sinner as well as the righteous. "Let all that you do be done with love" (1 Corinthians 16:14.).

People will always present challenges to us in our love walk. Remember, the unconditional love that God has for us should be the same love that we have for others. Love causes our relationships to bond, especially when there are wounded spirits. People are drawn to those who radiate a spirit of unconditional love, and this will surely immobilize the enemy. When we show love in our relationships, love will come back to us in some form or fashion. The more spiritual responsibility you acquire, the more love it takes to succeed. To whom much is given much is required. The enemy will often seek after those who consistently obey the commandments of love, which is the fulfilling of the whole law.

It is not very wise to respond to anger with more anger. When you respond to anger with empathy and love, you can often break the cycle of anger and hatred and convert even your enemies into friends. If we wish to be loved, we must give love, but keep in mind that the essence of love in not to receive it but to give it.

Walking in love puts us in a position to be protected by God; it puts us in the will of God. Love is a protective barrier. It ensures that God will be there to turn evil into good. Love is a part of the healing process that will bring restoration whether you are in the secular world or in the Christian environment. It empowers you to overcome opposition, it keeps you hoping and believing when others are becoming discouraged. Love cultivates a positiveness that can propel you to greater success in life.

God intended everything to be built on the foundation of love. Love forces out all acts of evil. Returning love instead of evil shows that you are not a victim. Responding in love will conquer all. Love never fails.

God assures us that, no matter what we are going through, we can walk in His perfect will for our lives and never doubt the power of love. God has destined and appointed us to come progressively to know His will; that is, to perceive, to recognize more strongly and clearly, and to become better and more intimately acquainted with Him.

Unless we stand up for what is good, nothing else we do will matter. Our true worth is the good we do in the world. We must be the change we wish to see in the world.

We are all unique individuals, created for special purposes. Become living examples of the God-kind of love in the lives of others.

As we face the inevitable challenges of life here on earth, we must equip ourselves with the commandments of love, and when we do, we can expect the best not only for today but for the future.

Releasing love in our circumstances breaks the power of the enemy and ensures that Satan will not defeat us or destroy our Christian relationships. No matter how horrible the pain of the circumstances, you'll find that the unconditional love for others is more powerful. *Love never fails.*

 *Chapter 2*

DON'T PUT YOUR CONFIDENCE IN MAN

Christian believers should put their confidence in God and not man. When you put your confidence in man, you dishonor God. God will never share His glory with man. Man can only be a vessel used by God. "It is better to trust in the Lord than to put confidence in man" (Psalm 118:8).

Your faith and confidence should be in one who will never fail you and who is always there. God is Jehovah-Shammah (God is there). Whenever you find yourself losing hope, God is always there. Put your trust and hope in the Lord. "Blessed is the man who trust in the Lord, and whose hope is in the Lord" (Jeremiah 17:7).

We must not lose confidence in trusting God, and we must not begin to trust in ourselves and what we can accomplish or what we can make happen. God's Word is filled with promises of strength and courage, but we can be strong and courageous only if we place our confidence in Him. The Lord has promised to keep everyone who trusts in Him and who has his or her mind focused on Him in perfect peace. "Thus, says the Lord: 'Cursed is the man who trusts in man and makes flesh his strength, whose heart departs from the Lord'" (Jeremiah 17:5).

God is always with us despite how we see our circumstances, despite how we react to our trials. Whatever you are going through, God is never far from you; He is always there. Trust God to work things out, and never let anything grow bigger than your faith in God. Nothing apart from God can save us or make us whole.

Don't let obstacles and circumstances deter your trust in God's power to overcome. Have unshakable faith and confidence in God. When we put our trust in God and His revealed Word, our lives will take on a new stability and focus.

Those new believers who observe your godly examples of doing things will see that trusting God's way of life produces good results.

New believers will also see that those Christian believers who trust in God must accompany the words they speak with their beliefs. We must accompany God's Word with deeds that match.

Those Christian believers who trust in God's Word are the ones who talk less and listen more. Also, it seems that those who are steadfast and strong in the Lord can withstand the ill comments that come their way. Trust God's promises to amend your relationship with others.

Trust is at the core of every relationship whether with God or man. Trust provides an environment of confidence in a relationship. Believers who exemplify character that trust in God will have positive interactions with others.

A relationship without trust lacks reliability and respect. Trust is having faith, it is a firm belief, you believe when you see no evidence. We must learn to trust God in every circumstance and in every area of our lives. "Do not put your trust in princes, nor in a son of man, in whom there is no help" (Psalm 146:3).

Those who put their confidence in government, finances, other people, or themselves will be disappointed in life, but those who put their confidence in God will never feel ashamed. When our confidence comes from anything other than God, it will fail.

If you make the Word the final authority in your life, it will give you stability. When everything else around you gives way, let what God's Word says settle the issues of life. You will be confident in God and His Word when others are confused, and you will be peaceful when others are under pressure.

When you have faith and confidence in the Word, you can have full assurance of eternal life. Your life will take on a new and exciting existence, one with open doors of unlimited opportunities.

Trusting God is one of the most important decisions that you can make for your life. When you trust God, your mind is at peace, you have no fears and worries. Your thinking is in line with the Word and what you believe will be right. If what you believe is right, then what you speak will be right.

If we put our trust in God, we will become strong, mature Christians. We can follow God in full confidence in His wisdom, power, and plan. And as we obey the Lord, He will give us anointings and spiritual gifts to meet the needs of others.

Trusting God to intervene in your hurtful situations will diminish those thoughts that keep us in bondage.

We put no confidence in our flesh, but we have every confidence in the God who made us, called us, saved us, and keeps us.

Confidence in man has limited potential, but confidence in God has unlimited possibilities. As Christians Believers, we should become spiritually aligned with the Word and place your hope and confidence in God. God has no record of failure. *Don't put your confidence in man.*

Chapter 3

FORGIVE AND FULFILL YOUR DESTINY

Gossip and slander often cause church hurts and have become so prevalent that they are rarely addressed in our Christian environments. Speaking falsely and revealing the private matters of others creates discord among Christian believers. Turn Satan down when he presents you with the temptation to gossip and slander in your Christian environments. "A false witness will not go unpunished, and he who speaks lies shall perish" (Proverbs 19:9).

In our Christian environment, it is inevitable that we will be hurt or feel mistreated in one way or another in our relationships. The pain of words spoken falsely penetrates deeply into our hearts simply because the pain is created by the people we love and trust. This makes it difficult to forgive and forget a transgression.

We may say that the hurt that we feel in our hearts is too great for us to forgive and let go of, but if we do not forgive, we will be tortured by that misdeed for the rest of our lives. Those who hurt us continue to cause us pain each time we remember the incident—until we release those people to God and forgive.

Christ died on Calvary to release us from any guilt, shame, condemnation, and unforgiveness, so He commands us to forgive as He forgave us. And it is only through forgiveness that we can be truly free—free to move forward unchained from our past to fulfill our destinies.

Releasing those who have wronged you is fundamental to receiving from God. You cannot expect your prayers to be answered and hold grudges in your hearts at the same time. "If I regard iniquity in my heart, the Lord will not hear" (Psalm 66: 18).

Forgiveness is the highest act of love; it releases without blame. Naturally, it goes against our human nature to behave positively toward someone we feel deserves punishment. But when Christian people treat you as those in the secular world, this is cause for concern. Forgiving those who have hurt you is the key to your healing and divine peace.

If your Christian sisters or brothers refuse to offer forgiveness of an offense toward you, you are still obligated to forgive them. Their failure to repent and forgive will have to be rectified between them and God. Unforgiveness opens the door for Satan to steal, kill, and destroy. The enemy is working overtime to stop you from fulfilling your destiny.

A spirit of resentment, bitterness, and anger keeps you under Satan's control. Don't allow the effects of inappropriate behavior to take root in your heart. A clear conscience will enable you to move forward in your relationships.

Remember that, behind every offense, is the adversary, the devil. His target is not the person who offended you; rather, his target is actually you, the victim of the offense. His plan is to get you to harbor anger and bitterness and open the door to unforgiveness. Forgiving is crucial to your own well-being.

Satan wants to make you feel as though you will lose something by forgiving, but really you have everything to gain and very little to lose. You gain peace, joy, love, and the acceptance of your heavenly Father. You lose the reoccurring torture of remembering the offense every time the thought of the person comes to mind.

When we hold unforgiveness in our hearts, our effectiveness as spiritual beings is diminished, our faith in the promises of God is diminished, and we are rendered powerless. Allow the healing process to begin by letting peace reign in your heart and mind. "Peace I leave with you, my peace I give to you; not as the world gives do I give to you. Let not your heart be troubled, neither let it be afraid" (John 14:27).

Healing is part of your inheritance. To be healed is your right through the Word of God and by the shed blood of Jesus.

Healing is an active, conscious process that can occur only when you allow yourself to feel the emotions, not repress them or hold them inside of you.

God has provided deliverance from the pain of church hurts; you only need to forgive. When you forgive, you are reaching out to a person and inviting him or her back into a former relationship. Forgiveness is just the beginning of a healing process. Just as your physical injuries take time to heal, so do your emotional injuries. Time enables the mind to process and move beyond the hurtful feelings. A forgiving heart is receptive to the plans and purposes of God.

Lack of forgiveness for others is not an option for Christian believers. Be more than just a person with position or title in our Christian environment. Be the person who can give spiritual guidance and restoration to others. "Brethren, if a man is overtaken in any trespass, you who are spiritual restore such a one in a spirit of gentleness, considering yourself less you also be tempted" (Galatians 6:1.).

In your conflicting circumstances, if you put yourself in the other person's place and contemplate how you would react or what you would say if you were in his or her position, you will see things more clearly. Looking at others' points of view always makes you change your initial reactions.

Remember there are no forces of darkness that God's Word cannot conquer. God's promises have an answer for every evil work. You can withstand the storms of life and live a life that is pleasing to God and thus pave the way to move forward to fulfill your destiny.

God has a plan for all our lives. He devises plans to strengthen us in our walk with Him, to develop our character, and to prepare us for our purpose. We need only to yield to the path He has chosen for us. God will never allow us to move to the next level of our destiny without first successfully passing our tests and trials. Like any finished product, we should be ready to perform after successful completion; therefore, we can move forward to what He has prearranged for us to do. "But he knows the way that I take; when He has tested me, I shall come forth as gold" (Job 23:10).

We will never understand the trials and pathways that lead us to fulfill our destiny. It is always beneficial to stay spiritually focused to get clear direction from God. He always makes us wait on His plan of action because His plan is perfect. He sees the beginning and the end. When we wait patiently for God, the outcome will always one that is beneficial.

Church hurts also occur when people display prideful attitudes. Pride creates division in our relationships.

Those who are prideful have a high self-regard and they are blind to their own weaknesses. They focus on title or position, they like the spotlight, they feel entitled, they point out the flaws in others and rarely admit their own flaws, they feel they have nothing to learn from others. If we humble ourselves and release the pride in our hearts, forgiveness becomes so much easier to handle.

When we learn how to die to the flesh and depend solely on our spirits to lead us, our misunderstandings, selfish acts, and prideful attitudes will cease to exist. Let the spirit inside of you control the outside spirit. Your power lies within.

Ask God if there is any unforgiveness toward others in your heart. Ask Him to help you to release them. See those Christian believers who cause harm as victims of Satan's manipulation to move you out of right standing with God. Choose to forgive because unforgiveness closes the door to eternal life. Matthew 6:14–15 tells us that, if you forgive the evildoing of others, your Heavenly Father will forgive your evildoing, but if you do not forgive the evildoing of others, neither will your Heavenly Father forgive your evildoing.

Do not tolerate long-range dissatisfaction, frustrations, and unforgiveness in your Christian environments. We must confront our problems sooner rather than later. The longer we harbor unforgiveness, the more difficult it becomes. Unforgiveness must be dealt with as soon as possible by repentance and through prayer. If the person you need to forgive is deceased, prayer is your only avenue to release the person you forgive and maintain a clear conscious.

Praying for our persecutors is one of the hardest tasks for Christian's believers to accomplish. We need help from God to accomplish this act of love. When we pray, we change the nature of that relationship from one of anger and bitterness to one of love and concern for the person. "And whenever you stand praying, if you have anything against anyone, forgive him; that your Father in heaven may also forgive you your trespasses" (Mark 11:25).

Pray and forgive the other person in faith because you cannot depend on your own feelings. Forgiveness frees you to live in the present, allowing you to move on, free from the bondage of an unforgiving heart. Pray this prayer:

> Father, in the Name of Jesus, I make a fresh commitment to you to live in peace and harmony, not only with my brothers and sisters of the Body of Christ but also with my friends and family members. I let go of all bitterness, resentment, envying, strife, and unkindness in any

form. I give no place to the devil, in Jesus's Name. I forgive and release all who have hurt me. From this moment on, I purpose to walk in love, to seek peace, to live in agreement, and to conduct myself toward others in a manner that is pleasing to you. In Jesus Name, I pray. Amen.

Prayer calms the spirit. It moves you to spiritual contentment and redirects your thoughts away from yourself. You cannot be consumed with anger and expect to have a pleasing relationship with God.

As long as our spirits are overflowing with the spiritual forces of love, joy, peace, patience, kindness, meekness, goodness, faithfulness, and self-control, Satan cannot deceive us. If God's Word is flowing in our hearts and minds, forgiving others will become second nature.

Moving beyond our hurts cannot be accomplished unless there is forgiveness that is brought about through unconditional love in a situation—a love that dispels any wrong doing, that finds no fault. The power of forgiveness and the power to heal are the same force. Without forgiveness, there can be no healing.

In many of our interactions, we don't realize how degrading our words can be toward others and how those words can cause unpleasant feelings in people's lives. Unpleasant words can destroy self-esteem, and false accusations can affect you emotionally as well as psychologically. Our behavior should be different from the behavior of those who imitate Satan.

Often, we make mountains out of molehills, and sometimes our unpleasant circumstances just require an understanding heart that can channel the situation into a solution that will benefit both parties. Displaying the heart of God in our situations will always guarantee the right outcome.

We know from experience that it is easier to criticize than to give correction; we also know that it is easier to find faults than solutions, and we realize that people who walk in righteousness will be criticized.

You can silence your critics not by arguing with them, not by defending yourself, but by keeping quiet and continuing to do good and inspire hope in others.

All who desire to live godly lives in Christ Jesus will suffer persecutions and afflictions. God's Word says that we should endure afflictions as a good soldier. God has provided a way of escape from our afflictions. Psalm 34:19 states that the righteous will receive numerous afflictions in life, but the Lord will set the righteous free from all of them.

You don't have to retaliate or match evil for evil in hurtful situations. God will repay you at the appointed time for whatever wrong you have done to one another.

Church hurts occur in so many different circumstances. Hurts come when we have conflicts with our Christian sisters and brothers over little insignificant things, when we make assumptions without having the facts, and when we see weaknesses in them and refuse to assist them. "We then who are strong ought to bear with the scruples of the weak, and not to please ourselves. Let each of us please his neighbor for his good, leading to edification" (Romans 15:1-2).

Envy and jealousy toward others cause church hurts; these are prevalent in our Christian environments. Know who you are and your purpose in life. If you know your identity, envy and jealousy will not affect you. We all have divine purposes and destinies. We all play important roles in the Body of Christ. God gave each of us spiritual gifts and anointings to do what no other person can do except us. God made us all unique and different.

You can eliminate most church hurts by being supportive of others in your Christian settings. When there is something lacking in a situation, be the one to fill in the gap. Be the one who can bring completion to a project or a task without a boastful attitude. Be the one who can make an impact on people lives without receiving recognition.

The church should be an environment of peace, tranquility, burden lifting, and yoke destroying—a place of worship. But instead it has become a place of hatred, disunity, and ridicule where people are hurting people, and no one is ever able to heal.

Forgiveness is a spiritual force that should be prevalent among Christians today. When situations occur that bring about emotional pain and hurt, we should be the ones to forgive quickly, remain positive, and retain cohesive Christian relationships with one another.

We all have spoken words of regret in our interactions with Christian friends and acquaintances; if you never make mistakes you cease to learn.

There is an old proverb that says if you have nothing good to say about a person, don't say anything. We must be cautious about the words we speak and the things we do in our Christian relationships.

God holds you accountable for your behavior and actions. Every careless word has a consequence. Decide to let go of that passive mentality that moves you into stagnation; instead, live a life that prepares and channels you to forgive and fulfill your destiny.

There are more and more people who are hurting and are never able to heal. The healing begins when there is forgiveness. Forgiveness enables the hurt partner to be freed from carrying the pain, anger, and bitterness. I don't claim that it is easy to forgive, but it is necessary; it is what God requires from us. The outcome will always be beneficial if we forgive. God takes great pleasure in those who cheerfully do His will.

Although, the world continues to change, God's love remains the same, and He is ready to comfort us and strengthen us whenever we turn to him.

You can be healed of hurtful situations as you surrender them to God, knowing that He is the one who can bring true liberty. There is healing for those who have experienced rejection, pain, and sorrow, and there is healing for those who have allowed bitterness and unforgiveness to take root in their hearts. "He heals the broken hearted and binds up their wounds" (Psalm 147:3).

You have been redeemed to become a vessel to be used for God's purposes. He bought you with a price on Calvary. You are not your own; your life belongs to God. Be a vessel of honorable use.

God has very important work for you to do—work that no one else on earth can accomplish the way you can. You must faithfully tackle the important work that God has placed before you.

We are called to be kernels of wheat that fall to the ground and die to themselves and enable God to bring forth new life. To forgive, we have to die to self, and only then will we be able to start anew in our relationships with God and man.

We are imperfect human beings. Most of us are easily angered, quick to blame, slow to forgive, and even slower to forget. Yet, as Christians, we are commanded to forgive others just as Christ has forgiven us. *Forgive and fulfill your destiny.*

Chapter 4

WISDOM—THE PRINCIPLE THING

In today's society, wisdom from God is paramount in order to succeed. When we are confronted with challenging situations, seek God's wisdom and trust it. When you do, you will receive untold blessings. "Wisdom is the principal thing; therefore, get wisdom. And in all your getting, get understanding" (Proverbs 4:7).

Leaders, whether in a ministry setting or in the secular world, should rely on wisdom in their leadership roles, making good judgement and quality decisions when confronted with life's challenges.

Christian leaders who communicate in an appropriate manner will usually make good, sound decisions in their leadership roles, and their actions usually line up with the truth. They make decisions that the Holy Spirit will act on, decisions that are acceptable. "The lips of the righteous know what is acceptable, but the mouth of the wicked what is perverse" (Proverbs 10:32).

Godly wisdom is an effective means for demonstrating effective leadership. Christian leaders who influence people and inspire change are the ones who use wisdom to persevere with great expectations in our Christian environments.

Be wise and prudent when you speak. Let well-chosen words come from your mouth. Make wise choices when faced with many paths of judgment, and don't allow your flesh to dictate your actions or attitudes.

Acknowledge negative behavior patterns and use them as opportunities to eradicate the plans of the enemy to move you into unrighteousness. Seek God's wisdom, which comes from above, and you will experience success in all your endeavors.

Those who imitate God can be the wisest people who walk the earth. They have the ability to discern or judge what is right, follow the soundest course of action, and make an impact not only in the Christian environment but in the world around them. Christian leaders should be the ones who set the standard in our Christian environments, showing good judgment in all that they do for the Lord—not with the wisdom of man but with the wisdom of God.

Christians leaders must seek the most effective means of communication using wise decision making. They must have the courage to speak the truth or bring correction to those things that are not of

God no matter what the circumstances. We should incorporate problem solving conversations in our relationships that will help us make well-informed decisions in our Christian environments.

We all have stumbled in many things in life and have said things that were unpleasant in our conversations, but speaking words that communicate in the right tone should be of utmost importance in our Christian environments. Know what to do and what to say when confronted with adversity. "I have taught you in the way of wisdom; I have led you in right paths. When you walk, your steps will not be hindered, and when you run, you will not stumble" (Proverbs 4:11–12).

When our spirits are wounded, we can seek wise counsel, and we must be willing to yield to the appropriate way to deal with our emotional pain. When people lie, disrespect you, belittle you, and wound you with words, the effects can have a lasting impact. You may feel disconnected or rejected, but you must not take it as a personal assault. This is the work of the enemy who wants to open the door to sin. With wise counsel, you will listen to those who encourage ways of doing and being right. "A wise man will hear and increase learning, and a man of understanding will attain wise counsel" (Proverbs 1:5).

Use wisdom by displaying self-control, understanding, and peace when offense comes, not only in words but also in actions. Repent of having offended anyone. Repent and turn away from speaking inappropriate words again. Offense is one of the most favorable weapons of the enemy. Our response to offence should one of composure. James 1:19–20 tells us that we should be quick to listen, slow to speak, and slow to become angry, because human anger does not produce the righteousness of God. When we are offended, anger should not be our first response.

Instructions from those who possess wisdom is needed in our relationships when our attitudes and the words we speak do not bring edification to the hearer. The only words that should be uttered are words that align with the will of God. We should never release the power and effects of hurtful words spoken over others, whether in our Christian relationships or in the secular environment. We must discipline ourselves to speak in a way that conveys respect, gentleness, and humility.

The wisdom of God often places us in positions in the church environments where we are not comfortable. He moves us to places that will challenge us and to places that will increase our knowledge and intimacy with Him—places that will lead us into our purpose and destinies. God is continuously molding us and shaping us into vessels to be used by Him. We are a work in progress.

When you rely on the wisdom of God, you don't have to face the day-to-day challenges in our Christian or secular environments without making sensible decisions and right choices. Wisdom always waits for the right time to act, while emotions always push for immediate action.

God is never far removed from us. He is always with us, always willing to calm the storms of life, always willing to give a word to the wise. Remember, Proverbs 15:3 reminds us that God is always there keeping watch over the evil and the good.

We must realize that it is never enough simply to hear the wise instructions of God; we must also live by them. Adhere to instructions that will lead you to make wise choices that will move you into a life that is pleasing to God.

Speak words of wisdom that bring healing and peace to those around you. When you do, you receive the peace and tranquility that only God can give. Do not be wise in your own eyes. Do not lean to your own understanding. Rather, use the wisdom discerned from above. "But the wisdom that is from above is first pure, then peaceable, gentle, willing to yield, full of mercy and good fruits, without partiality and without hypocrisy" (James 3:17).

Wisdom is the means by which we can give directions in our difficult circumstances to accomplish the best results. Wisdom is also the ability to recognize and judge what is applicable for your life.

Wisdom should be foremost among our Christian believers in the work they have been called to do. God said, in James 1:5, that, if any of you lacks wisdom, ask God. He gives it to all freely, and without finding fault, He will give it to you.

Your life has a purpose that was ordained by God before you were formed in your mother's womb. He set you apart, consecrated you, and appointed you to serve his purposes. God freely gives each of us wisdom and provision to carry out those plans that He has ordained from the beginning. He has plans to prosper you and not to harm you.

Remember, a wise Christian rises above unpleasant circumstances. And God often works through our circumstances in revealing His perfect will for our lives. *Wisdom—the principle thing.*

Chapter 5

OBEDIENCE IS BETTER THAN SACRIFICE

When we honor those whom God has placed in authority over us, we maintain a good conscience. Submission to God will always conform to submission to those in authority. "Obey those who rule over you, and be submissive, for they watch out for your souls, as those who must give account. Let them do so with joy and not with grief, for that would be unprofitable for you" (Hebrews 13:17).

Obedience demonstrates compliance to instructions or commands of God and those in authority. Make every effort to follow through to what is right according to the Word of God in order to be led in the right direction. Loss of direction and purpose in life may indicate the problem of an undesirable relationship to God-given authority. God has a plan for our lives, and it involves submission to obtain clear direction. Those who pursue their own desires may delay God's purposes for their lives.

There are more and more people in the world today who are constantly moving in the opposite direction of heartfelt devotion and obedience to God. If we diligently obey the voice of the Lord our God and observe all His commands, we will experience all the blessings that He has bestowed upon us. God has promised us blessings for obedience, as stated in Deuteronomy 28:1.

Church hurts occur when there is a termination or dismissal in the workplace by Christian believers who do not comply to those in authority, consequently, creating a loss of employment. Our failure to cooperate when dismissed in the work environment will ultimately result in emotional distress, heartache, and an unpleasantness for all parties involved.

Also, refusing to assist in the replacement of our successors is not justification for having been dismissed. If we cooperate and assist our successors, the tension and humiliation of the situation will be eased. Disregard your own feelings and make an effort to bring harmony and peace in the situation.

You sometimes may feel that those in authority have treated you unfairly. This is not justification to repay evil for evil. We are not God's appointed judges to return evil for evil. There is nothing to gain from retaliating actions. If we do this, we have played subtly into the enemy's hand, because this is a tactic of the enemy to lead us down a path to lose our dignity or respect. "Repay no one evil for evil. Have regard for good things in the sight of all men" (Romans 12:17).

Reject any misconduct or inappropriate behavior that results in noncompliance of those in authority. See the error of your ways and acknowledge your mistakes. God will forgive you, heal you, and make you whole again.

Sometimes we may feel that, when we submit to authority, we may discover that obedience can seem costly. There will be some situations in which obedience requires you to let go of your own rights.

Walking in obedience to those whom God has placed in authority will bring favor to aid you in your time of need. Your reward for obedience is far greater than any difficulties you may be experiencing.

All too often, we convey the wrong attitude, and consequently we regret words spoken in anger in our dismissals. It is always better to go in peace rather than to speak of dissatisfaction of others. It is also beneficial to us when we leave a workplace to convey an attitude that will welcome our return. Our attitude should be one that is submissive even in the face of unfavorable conditions.

Standing strong and walking uprightly when you have been removed or terminated in a church environment requires courage and humility. It indicates that you know who you are and that you have confidence in the Word of God that all things will work in your favor for those who love God and obey His Word. "He who heeds the word wisely will find good, and whoever trusts in the Lord, happy is he" (Proverbs 16:20).

Negative feelings can cause hurts to occur in our Christian environments. Negative anger can result when leaders' and administrators' responsibilities become overly numerous. Understandably, people can easily become overwhelmed with ministry tasks that cause them to speak negatively toward others. Anger can lead a person to the point of having ill feeling toward those who are in authority over you; consequently, this creates displeasure in your work relationships.

When you are overwhelmed and tempted to take matters into your own hands, dismiss those feelings that dictate inappropriate desires or ungodly behavior. The battle is not yours; the battle is the Lord's.

Entrust yourself to the one who judges righteously, and by these actions you will win every battle.

Church hurts also occur when we are confronted with unpleasant situations and hurtful remarks by those in authority. Additionally, there may be a misuse of authority by leaders and administrators. If they use wisdom in their decisions with good sound judgment and knowledge of what is reasonable in their interactions, this will bring about obedience and a right relationship with God and man.

When you are given authority, it is not the right to do what you want. Actually, you have the power to do what is right.

Stand on God's Word with confidence that He will handle any misuse of authority that may appear in the Body of Christ. God is more than able and willing to turn your hurts into actions that will destroy the plans of the enemy in our Christian relationships.

Show obedience by humbling yourself. True humility is to recognize that our opinions or circumstances are of less importance than the opinions or circumstances of others. Humility moves us to forget about our feelings and focus on the circumstances and needs of others. Humility dispels anger and heals wounds; it moves us forward to a reasonable solution of action.

To have done what is right in the sight of God is far more rewarding than to do wrong and suffer emotionally. "To do righteous and justice is more acceptable to the Lord than sacrifice" (Proverbs 21:3).

When your thoughts and attitudes are of a spiritual nature, you can endure any circumstances that bring challenges to your life. Christian believers must continue to walk in obedience to avoid sorrows and trust God to make the pathway smooth.

Tests and trials are inevitable. We will be tested to see if our hearts are ready to move to the next level. Many of the situations we face in life are just preparation for kingdom building. Flushing out impurities and flaws is part of God's plan to lead us to the good life that He has prearranged for us to live.

Every experience God gives us, every person He brings into our path, every trial is just preparation for our future that only He can see. Christian trials and experiences are just preparation for God-given assignments, so don't lose heart at any of your tribulations. God uses tests and trials to strengthen our dependence on Him. Trust God to deliver you in your trials. Your misfortunes may be blessings in disguise. "Therefore, I ask that you do not lose heart at my tribulations for you, which is your glory" (Ephesians 3:13).

We should rejoice and pray when confronted with circumstances that cause church hurts. Rejoicing demonstrates that we have faith in God and we believe the Word of God when we see no evidence of it. We pray for the person or circumstances because prayer brings restoration and healing.

In our Christian relationships, we will either make or break a situation with our reactions. Reactions that originate from our natural senses are always contrary to the word of God. We will always be confronted by negative reactions and conflict with people. Be the one to turn negatives into positives, be the one to create an atmosphere of harmony and unity in your Christian relationships.

The consequences of disobedience are never good. We must eliminate those spirits of rebellion and self-righteousness. They will only lead us down the path of destruction. "If you are willing and obedient, you shall eat the good of the land, but if you refuse and rebel, you shall be devoured by the sword, for the mouth of the Lord has spoken" (Isaiah 1:19–20).

It doesn't matter what misfortunes we experience. It doesn't matter if there is a financial lost. What matters is that God will reward your obedience when you submit and surrender to Him. Your obedience guarantees favor from God.

Walking in obedience to God pays with blessings that will last a life time. *Obedience is better than sacrifice.*

Chapter 6

SPIRITUAL GROWTH AND STABILITY

Spiritual growth and stability in our church environments are enhanced by Christians who have allowed the Word of God to dwell in their hearts richly. Their spirits are strengthen, and they move forward without regard to adversity or feelings of inadequacy. They can manage the most confused situations in a calm and composed manner.

Acquiring spiritual growth and stability is a necessity in our Christian environments. Spiritually mature Christians are constantly increasing in the knowledge of the Word of God. And the greater our knowledge of the Word, the higher our level of ministry responsibility. From everyone who has been given much, much will be demanded; and from the one who has been entrusted with much, much more will be asked (Luke 12:48).

To test your spiritual growth and stability, to see if you are making any progress, examine how you communicate with others in love. One of the most important characteristics of believers who are maturing and growing in Christ is their love for God and their love for one another. Mature Christians have the courage to face the truth. They care about what is on the inside—in the spirit—more than they care about outer appearances. If the inside is right—heart, emotions, faith—then the outside will fall into place. They are led by the spirit of God. They practice what they preach and spend quality time with God.

Christian maturity leads us outward, away from ourselves, and into paths of service and ministry to others. Every time you make the choice to serve others, you will grow up a little more into the image of Christ. You will leave spiritual infancy behind and take another step toward spiritual maturity.

One of the ultimate purposes in the Body of Christ is to establish growth and stability for equipping the saints for the work of the ministry. Be diligent to do the work of the Lord so that the work that God wants us to perform through the local church can be accomplished.

As Christian believers, we have been entrusted by God to fulfill our assignments and purposes here on earth. God will work out everything for our good and for the good of the ministry when we equip ourselves to fulfill His purposes. "And we know that all things work together for good to those who love God, to those who are called according to His purpose" (Romans 8:28).

God's desire for you is to grow spiritually, obey His commandments and statutes, and trust in His directions as you seek His will for your lives. Make the most of every possible opportunity to renew your mind with the Word of God.

Constantly seeking God's presence will bring about a spiritual discernment of both good and evil so that you will know what is best. "But solid food belongs to those who are full age, that is, those who by reason of use have their senses exercised to discern both good and evil" (Hebrews 5:14).

A Christian believer who seeks daily to please God in everything and who strives for spiritual growth through prayer and staying connected to God by imitating Him will gain victory over every battle.

As we are striving for spiritual maturity, offense is inevitable, but we have dominion over the enemy. Mature Christians are not offended when immaturity is displayed in our Christian environments. The higher you climb spiritually, the greater the opposition.

One way to combat offenses from people is just simply learn to just respond to ungodly comments with no response at all. When you don't give feedback to criticism, people will soon stop talking or the conversation will end. "Where there is no wood, the fire goes out; and where there is no talebearer, strife ceases" (Proverbs 26:20).

We attain spiritual growth and stability through a continuous learning process; it doesn't happen overnight. Don't become stagnant. Be a river, not a swamp. A swamp is stagnant because it collects and retains water. Let God's Word flow like a river. The Bible says that rivers of living waters will flow from the heart of those who believe in Him (John 7:38). Don't live your life from month to month and year to year in the same circumstances, never changing, never increasing in the Word of God, and never moving forward in life. Keep your soul nourished by letting the Word flow like a river.

Encourage spiritual growth by speaking words that inspire and motivate others. As you build them up, your own spirit will become stronger. Strong spirits can resist the attack of the enemy.

Christian believers can grow spiritually also by learning from one another in our strengths and weaknesses, in our good times and our hard times, in our achievements and failures. Learning to endure when things look bad has always been a great challenge for mankind. Making the right decisions is easy when things are going great, but when the enemy throws a fiery dart, it will become far more difficult. Whether it is within the church walls or with family and friends or with coworkers, a mature Christian will always find the right path to amend differences.

Sometimes our hurts derive from misinterpreting the words or actions of people in our Christian relationships. Conflicts are created. Our conflicts are not designed to break us, but to strengthen us in the spiritual role God has destined for us to follow. If all conflicts, struggles, and sufferings were eliminated, our spirits would not reach maturity.

Associate with fellow believers who, by their words and actions, encourage spiritual growth. The people you associate with should be like-minded. Your associations will determine what you believe. What you believe is what you become.

If you guard your tongue in all circumstances with positive words, you will indeed demonstrate maturity. When you have been firmly rooted and built up in God's Word and established in your faith, spiritual maturity will abound. "As you have therefore received Christ Jesus the Lord, so walk in in Him, rooted and built up in Him and established in the faith, as you have been taught, abounding in it with thanksgiving" (Colossians 2:6–7).

Without spiritual growth and stability, people would not be transformed or matured into the place God has destined them to be. God never calls us without enabling us. If He calls you to do something, He makes it possible for you to do it.

In our growth process, living a life with a consistent spiritual walk with God greatly influences those we witness to. In our desire to share the gospel, we may be the only example of Jesus someone will ever see.

Stay connected to the power source—the supernatural power of God. With this power we can give people hope for the future and comfort them in their afflictions. We should be the ones who instill confidence in God in their lives, and we should be the ones who meet the needs of the people within the communities. "Remember the word to your servant, upon which you have caused me to hope. This is my comfort in my affliction, for your word has given me life" (Psalm 119: 49–50).

Meeting the real needs of the people requires a level of maturity in Christian believers that only God can provide. But when we, as Christians, come into the knowledge of the truth, then God expects us to grow up spiritually and walk in the light of the truth of His Word.

We are like seeds planted in the ground that grow constantly as they are watered—a little at a time until we accomplish what we were created to be. Likewise, achieving spiritual growth and stability comes as we constantly keep the Word in our mouth and in The midst of our heart. *Spiritual growth and stability.*

Chapter 7

GOD IS OUR ONE AND ONLY SOURCE

In our Christian environments, many Christian believers have experienced church hurts when there is an unexpected crisis present in their lives. The expectation is that the church will be a source of comfort and to help in a time of need.

People carry the hurt when church leaders and members do not reach out to help them when they are faced with hardships and difficult times. They become angry and disappointed that their Christian leaders didn't respond with provisions when they needed them the most.

When you are tempted to contemplate the disappointments and the hurt that is felt during a crisis, look to the one who has all power. Don't let the tough times defeat you. God has already given you everything that you need for life and godliness.

Christian believers who have been faced with a lack of church response during a time of crisis should rely on God who is their provider in times of unexpected misfortune. Philippians 4:6–8 advises us not to anxious about anything. We should just make our requests known to God in prayer, give thanks to God, and let the peace of God guard our hearts and minds through Christ Jesus.

One of the greatest hindrances to not receiving from God is dependence on other sources. God will always make a way of escape in our desperations. Christian believers should always look to God as their source and only source. When you are in a situation when God is all you have, you soon discover He is all you really need.

When you are dependent on a source that fails, you become angry and very disappointed having critical thoughts and unloving attitudes. We should face our disappointments and trails of every sort by casting our cares to God and rely on Him to deliver us from our circumstances.

A well-known strategy of Satan is to lead you down a path of dependency on people and nullify your dependence on God. God's Word says that He will never leave us nor forsake us (Hebrews 13:5). God will deliver us in times of uncertainty when we call upon Him. Focus on God's unlimited possibilities. He has all sufficiency for all of life's difficulties.

In 2 Corinthians 9:8, we learn that our God is all sufficient, and He makes all grace abound toward us that we will always have our needs met in all things that we may continue to minister in every good work.

When we don't rely on God, we place limits on ourselves. There are no limits with God. We can either be containers that are limited by our own capacities, or we can be rivers that allow God's unlimited supply to flow continuously.

God is a jealous God. He does not want anyone taking His place in our lives as the provider. God is able to change our circumstances on our behalf in all our affairs.

When Christian leaders intentionally overlook a believers' plight, this will indeed cause hurtful feelings among the victims. But you must acknowledge your negative attitude and dependency on people before God by forgiving and having faith that God will supply all your needs. You will move past the heartache and eventually move past the pain.

We will always be confronted with times of misfortunate and crisis in our lives. Sometimes we have to face the harsh realities in life that are no fault of our own. But we have the victory when we call upon God in prayer. "Blessed be God, who has not turned away my prayer, Nor His mercy from me!" (Psalm 66:20). Pray this prayer, inserting words that reflect your personal concerns:

> Father, I ask you to forgive me. I thought negatively about _____ regarding my misfortune. I have been angry about it, and I have spoken angry words. I've harbored bitterness in my heart toward _____, and I

don't want it to go any further. Remove
this root of bitterness from me. Restore
me with a heart like yours. In Jesus's
name. Amen.

Obtain a clear conscience and remove hurt feelings
that hinder blessings and healing. God knows your
needs even before you ask. Through prayer, He can
restore your heart to one that gives you assurance
and peace of mind.

When you harbor bitter feelings toward those you
feel should aid you in your crisis, it shows that
you are dependent on their abilities. Having bitter
feelings, you tend to turn your thoughts within and
look only at your own circumstances. Instead, turn
your frustrations into faith in God, believing in His
abilities.

One way to get rid of ill feelings is to focus our attention on the needs of others; then we soon forget about our own needs. If we turn our attention to what we can give, then we will never be in lack. "He who gives to the poor will not lack, but he who hides his eyes will have many curses" (Proverbs 28:27).

Christian believers naturally look to their own church to help in troubling times, especially when they have spent many years giving of their tithes and offerings in their local ministry and faithfully serving the Lord.

Allow God to touch the hearts and minds of people to aide you during your crisis. See God as the one who is continuously loving you in your suffering and making provisions for you through others. This will ease the tension of many of our church hurts in our Christian environments.

God is our source for all our needs. People can be used only to transfer the blessings of the Lord from one person to another. Never rely on people as your source. God is our one and only source.

Our Christian environments and relationships can yield the most wonderful blessings in our lives while, at the same time, they can be the hardest challenges that we will ever face.

If God has the power to create and sustain the universe, He is more than able to sustain you during your difficult times.

Focus your eyes on the one who never changes instead of dwelling on your ever-changing circumstances. In our ever-changing circumstances of life, there is a never-changing God in control. There isn't a detail that escapes His eyes, a trial that doesn't touch

His heart, or a single experience that is beyond His compassion.

As a born-again believer, you have been given authority to use the name of Jesus, and His name is above all names. Jesus freely gave us this authority to those who believe in Him. The same spiritual qualities and the same authority inside Jesus is inside you. You have the permission and authority to go to the throne boldly and ask God to supply your needs. "Let us come boldly to the throne of grace, that we may obtain mercy and find grace to help in time of need" (Hebrews 4:16).

God's promises will cover every imaginable situation in your life, and every promise is available to you by faith. Thus, you can speak and cause things to happen. Every spiritual blessing has already been established for the believer as stated in Ephesians 1:3 to be received by faith.

Our lives are not determined by what happens to us, but by how we react to what happens, not by what life brings to us, but by the attitude we bring to life. A positive attitude during a crisis causes a chain reaction of positive thoughts, events, and outcomes.

No matter what unfortunate circumstances you find yourself in today, let people see you as one with total and complete confidence in God as your only source, and let them see you spiritually anchored in times of crisis. *God is our one and only sources.*

 *Chapter 8*

THERE IS NOTHING THAT YOU CANNOT OVERCOME

Life can be difficult and discouraging at times, but during our darkest moments, we can depend upon God. When we do, we find the courage to face even the most difficult circumstances with hearts full of hope.

Whatever we are going through or experiencing, God's Word can turn our despairs into hope. Bad situations can become good, and failures can become successes. When we are troubled, faith in God's Word will lead us to victory every time. "The righteous are delivered from trouble, and it come to the wicked instead" (Proverbs 11:8).

Remember, there's no situation so dark and so cleverly designed by the forces of evil that there is not a workable solution that will unlock it. There is an answer to your difficult situation.

We all have experience failure in our lives. Every adversity, every heartache is temporary, quitting last a life time. Failure in life is a necessary stepping stone to success. When you refuse to give up on life, that's when incredible things happen. Nothing in life that's worthwhile will come easy.

If you are harboring ill feelings toward others, it's time to forgive and move on. Move on to reap the abundance of blessings that God has planned for your life.

Don't ignore warning signs that tell you to turn from your wicked ways. When we confess our wrong attitudes with a true heart of repentance, we have the chance to start anew in our relationships.

Christ has given each of us grace and mercy to overcome in every area that Satan has so cleverly strategized for our failure. God redeemed the sins of His people with the sacrificial lamb of God—Jesus—so that you could become free of sin and total deliverance from the works of Satan. Coming clean about your wrongdoing and acknowledging your sin is the way back to a right relationship with God.

God does not deal with us in judgement; rather, He deals with us in mercy and grace. No matter how far we stray into darkness, the moment we call on His name, He is there to forgive us and put us back where we, as His children, belong—saved, delivered, and restored.

Whatever hurtful acts our Christian believers intended, the spirit of God can completely turn it around in our favor. Not surprisingly, very often it is the Christian believers who will criticize you most harshly rather than those in the secular world. "But as for you, you meant evil against me; but God meant it for good, in order to bring it about as it is this day, to save many people alive" (Genesis 50:20).

The pain that we have suffered in our trials will become avenues for healing. In the very places where we have been wounded, God's Word can bring healing and deliverance. "The Lord upholds all who fall and raises up all those who are bowed down" (Psalm 145:14).

Don't let a person's ungodly actions continue to remain in your thought life.

Change your thought life by letting go of negative thinking toward each other. The enemy attacks by feeding us negative thoughts. Not controlling your negative thought life will make you a defeated Christian. Take every thought captive to the obedience of Christ. Stop paying attention to what he or she did. Instead, undermine his or her efforts by forgiving and forgetting and moving on to fulfill your destiny.

No matter what your current relationship with God today, know that He hears you when you call upon Him. His love for you is immeasurable far beyond what you can comprehend. God loves you more than you will ever truly imagine.

One of the greatest comforters we have as born-again Christians is the person of the Holy Spirit who has come to dwell inside of us. He comforts us, instructs us, directs us. He prepares us to fulfill our destiny.

Storms may come. Don't fix your eyes on the storms, but see past them, and you will find strength and courage in their midst. Stand strong when adversity comes. Keep saying what God's Word says and keep doing what God's Word says to do. Continue to act on the written Word of God. "The way of the Lord is strength for the upright, but destruction will come to the workers of iniquity" (Proverbs 10:29).

Never give place to regrets and shame. Even if you did not succeed in previous attempts, don't lose heart. Don't give up. Giving up was never God's plan for our lives. There is no heart beyond God's reach. "I called on the Lord in distress; The Lord answered me and set me in a broad place" (Psalm 118:5).

Concealing deep-seated hurts from the past, pretending that all is well with your soul, and trying to hold on to a life full of bad choices is no way to live. Turn to God—the very one who can sustain you. Don't stop trusting in the one who has all power. We can be healed of our broken hearts and set free from oppression.

We must search our hearts to find the very source of our pain. You can't address a problem that you won't acknowledge. Confront those feelings. It isn't about changing the person who hurt you; it's about understanding yourself deep down inside in a more healing way.

If we hurt someone's feelings because we spoke too harshly to them or didn't speak to them at all, we can't excuse ourselves by saying, "I didn't even realize I offended her." As soon as you recognize that your words cause harm, apologize. Don't let a hurtful act linger.

We can overcome destructive criticism by changing our response to one of a positive nature. By changing our attitudes to respond positively, we can ease the tension and resolve our differences. I know this may be easier said than done, but as we strive to turn negatives into positives, we are guaranteed a favorable outcome. The decision to stay the course will bring the desired results.

Satan can invade your territory only when your actions are contrary to the Word of God. You have to make a quality decision to derail Satan's influence in your life. Satan will attack whomever will give him access.

To be delivered and set from the power of Satan sometimes requires a higher power.

If you sincerely want to be healed of an unforgiving heart, the power of God will help you to overcome. And when the power of God gets involved, you can rest assured that you will be delivered and set free.

God will give you every possible chance to respond to your adverse circumstances as He would with a forgiving heart—make a decision to not be under the control of Satan because his mode of operation is to steal, kill and destroy.

We can change our atmosphere around us by loving, blessing and speaking words of encouragement. Living our lives with a greater measure of God's love is very powerful. As Christians we should pray for those who curse us, love and not judge, be humble as opposed to proud and arrogant and forgive those who offend us. Show love in your relationships and watch the power of God change your circumstances.

In our own strength, we may try to forgive someone over and over again, only to call to mind the offense later. We must rely on God to purge our hearts through prayer.

Pray a prayer to release the hurt feelings in your relationships. Break the power of the enemy over your life. Pray this prayer:

> Father, thank you for healing me right now of those hurtful words. I ask you to touch my heart. As an act of my will, I choose not to be hurt. I release the hurt, the rejection, and the emotional pain in this relationship. Thank you, Father, for the freedom and the flow of the Holy Spirit touching my heart and mind right now. I take it by faith, and I'm healed in my heart, my mind, and my soul. In Jesus's Name, I pray. Amen!

Remember, to forgive is a personal choice we make. It's not about the person who hurt you. It is a choice you make to bring healing to yourself. It is about taking control of thoughts and emotions and not playing the part of a victim.

Christ-like behavior is a contradiction to the ways of the world. It goes against the grain from beginning to end. From the day that you were born-again until the day that you go to heaven to be with the Lord, you must stand against the current of a world always going the wrong way.

Keep in mind that our values and integrity are always on display, and our tongues will bring either healing or destruction. Bring your tongue in line with the Word of God. Reverse the enemy's attacks and make your enemies your friends.

Church hurts have been around for a long time among Christian believers and in our Christian environments. We experience hurts also in our everyday life with family members, relatives, friends, coworkers, and casual acquaintances. It is one of Satan's strategies to keep people in opposition with each other or to bring division in our relationships.

As you move closer and closer to fulfilling the call God has on your life, there will always be countless opportunities to lose your temper over trivial things. The enemy's job is to derail you from your purpose. Words that degrade and inconsiderate comments or remarks that indicate dislike should not be named among us.

Church hurts also occur to people who have been labeled as outcasts, who feel they don't belong in our Christian environments, who feel they don't measure up to our standards. They don't look like us, or they don't belong in our circles. Refusing to communicate and love people who don't think like you or agree with your methods create hurtful feelings. We must be a comfort to those who have experienced rejection and ridicule in our Christian environments. "Blessed be the God and Father of our Lord Jesus Christ, the Father of mercies and God of all comfort. Who comforts us in all our tribulations that we may be able to comfort those who are in any trouble, with that comfort with which we ourselves are comforted by God" (2 Corinthians 1:3–4).

There is nothing that can't be overcome in our Christian relationships. Be the one to welcome those who are rejected in our society, whose values maybe contrary the Word of God. It is our job to change bad behavior, hatred, anger, resentment, and bitterness. Ask God to enable you to use words as instruments of His love and grace. Take the initiative to treat each other fairly, reframe from favoring one group over another. It is our job to revive those who have been wounded by Christian believers.

We do not have to agree with the what people might believe or support, but God has commanded us to love others with an unconditional love just as He did.

When you are determined that Satan's plots of attack will no longer control your life, then you exert your God-given authority to override the forces of evil and darkness that so easily beset us.

Now more than ever, we need to speak words that will bring God's love to a hurting world. God wants us to be free from the emotional wounds of our past caused by hurtful words and actions. "Let no corrupt word proceed out of your mouth, but what is good for necessary edification, that it may impart grace to the hearers" (Ephesians 4:29).

If you have been wounded or rejected by uncaring Christian believers and leaders, don't be discouraged. Face the circumstances that are the greatest sources of your pressure. Overcome the situations that have overwhelmed you. Let people see you as a conquer.

As Christian believers, our primary responsibility is to bring people into a right relationship with God, not reject them as unfit for the kingdom. Mend the brokenhearted, build up those who are weak, welcome those who have been pushed away by Chrisitianity. Be a light in a world of darkness. Every problem has a solution. Every pain has a purpose. Every past has a future.

In this shifting, changing world that we live in, God is continually processing us to be imitators of Him. The key is to not become discouraged while we are in the process of being completed, but to remind yourself that God wants to move you forward to greater works.

Continue to do good, and when all the foolish hurtful words have faded away, you will be still standing strong.

Be the change that you want to see in the world. Change your spiritual atmosphere by walking in love in all your relationships victoriously. Just like walking outside of love will hurt people, walking in love can heal them.

God loves the afflicted as much as He loves the proud. He loves the rich as much as He loves the poor. He shines His grace upon us all. No crime exceeds God's compassion; no sin surpasses His love. "You have forgiven the iniquity of your people; you have covered all their sin" (Psalm 85:2).

As a born-again believer, there is nothing that you cannot overcome. What we acknowledge as hopeless, God declares as overcomeable. God accepts us wherever we are; He takes us through a cleansing process to mold and shape us to whom He has called us to be—vessels to be used by Him. "For whatever is born of God overcomes the world. And this is the victory that has overcome the world—our faith" (1 John 5:4).

You have the power to shape your destiny. The choices you make, whether good or bad, will determine the outcome. Ask God to help you to see the good in your trials and tribulations. If God has plans to greatly use you in the lives of others, you can expect your trials to be even greater than those of others.

God intends to use you in wonderful unexpected ways. He desires to lead you along a path of His choosing. Your role is to follow His lead. Don't let Satan hinder you from experiencing new and exciting things in your life.

Today, as you live in the present and look to the future, remember that God has amazing plans for you. God created you for a very important reason and has important work for you to do.

You can look to the future with hope because, one day, there will be no more heartache, no more rejection, no more separation, and no more suffering in your Father's house.

And remember, no problem is too big for God—and that includes yours. *There is nothing that you cannot overcome.*

CPSIA information can be obtained
at www.ICGtesting.com
Printed in the USA
BVHW070154231118
533755BV00009B/98/P